ME...
of
WINE

Edited by
Jeffrey Young

Author: Allegra Strategies
Design: John Osborne
Researcher: Olivia Renaud
Publisher: Allegra Publications Ltd

Visit our website:
meaningofeverything.com

Published by *Allegra* PUBLICATIONS Ltd © 2015

Walkden House, 10 Melton Street, London, NW1 2EB, UK

Dedicated to
Marlene & Maggie,
Fay & John,
Marcus & Elaine,
Ludovic & Ermina.

I can only please one
person per day.
Today is my day.

A meal without wine is called breakfast.

One kind word can change
someone's entire day.

Wine is constant proof
that God loves us and loves
to see us happy.

BENJAMIN FRANKLIN

Hocus pocus, I need wine
to focus.

I vow to drink more wine
so that I can do something
crafty with the corks.

A laugh is a smile
that bursts.

Sip happens.

Wine improves with age.
The older I get
the more I like it.

Don't forget to buy a bottle for Mum on Mother's Day. Remember, you're the reason she drinks.

Insanity is hereditary.
You get it from your children.

SAM LEVENSON

Alcohol:
Liquid confidence.

Drinking rum before 10am
makes you a pirate,
not an alcoholic.

A good man can make you
feel sexy, strong and able
to take on the world.
Oh sorry that's wine...

Who keeps putting
vegetables in the
wine crisper?

Wine is 'win' with an 'e'
on the end.

I cook with wine. Sometimes I even add it to the food.

W.C. FIELDS

If he was half as funny
as he thinks he is,
he would be twice as
funny as he really is.

Never laugh at your wife's
choices, you are one
of them.

Wine is for people who
can afford to lose a few
brain cells.

Oh, if I offended you with my opinion, you should hear the ones I keep to myself.

The secret to enjoying wine:

1. Open the bottle.

2. Let it breathe.

3. If it does not look like
it's breathing,
give it mouth to mouth.

Nobody cares if you are miserable, so you might as well be happy.

Men are like fine wine.
They start out as grapes.
It is our job to stamp all over
them until they mature into
something you would like
to have dinner with.

No woman has ever shot
a man while he was
washing the dishes.

I don't have a problem
with alcohol.
I have a problem
without alcohol.

Girl in bar:
'You remind me
of my next boyfriend.'

I never drink unless
I am alone or
with somebody.

I love you more than red wine, but please don't make me prove it.

I'm not arguing with you.
I am simply explaining
why I am right.

If anyone says that you drink too much on the weekends, stop talking to them. You don't need that kind of negativity around you.

If I had to live my life
again, I'd make the same
mistakes, only sooner.

TALLULAH BANKHEAD

True love isn't a big thing.
It's a million little things.

Alcohol.

Because no great story

starts with a salad.

Never look down on anybody unless you're helping them up.

JESSE JACKSON

If I drink too much wine,
I am an alcoholic.
But if I drink a lot of
Fanta, does that make me
fantastic?

A woman drove me to drink and I never had the decency to thank her.

W.C. FIELDS

Alcohol.

Some of the best times

you will never remember.

I'm sotally tober.

My doctor advised me not to drink every day, so I drink every night.

Whisky is risky.

Wine is sublime.

To alcohol!
The cause of –
and solution to –
all of life's problems.

HOMER SIMPSON

You can never start
a new chapter of your life
if you keep re-reading
the last one.

Dear wine, I saw the video.
You promised to make me
funnier, sexier, smarter
and a better dancer.
We need to talk.

One of the disadvantages
of wine is that it makes a
man mistake words
for thoughts.

SAMUEL JOHNSON

My drinking team
has a hockey problem.

Be a Fruit Loop
in a wonderful world
of Cheerios.

A bottle a day keeps the salary away!

I don't have
a drinking problem...
I'm actually quite good
at it.

I put my phone
on airplane mode,
but it doesn't fly.

One tequila,
two tequila,
three tequila,
floor.

Veni, Vidi, Vino.
I came, I saw, I wined.

When I read about the
evils of drinking wine,
I gave up reading.

Wine.
How classy people
get wasted.

Does running to the wine shop count as your daily workout?

Please keep drinking.
I have heard wine
makes me sexy.

The problem with the world is that everyone is a few drinks behind.

HUMPHREY BOGART

I'm not a wine lover.
I'm a frustrated
grape hater.

Be yourself.

Everybody else is taken.

The best things in life
aren't things.

Novinophobia: The fear of running out of wine.

Most smiles are started
by another smile.

Don't wait for the perfect
moment. Take the moment
and make it perfect.

Life is a waste of time.
Time is a waste of life.
Get wasted all the time and
you'll have the time
of your life.

BILLY CONNOLLY

Alcohol, taken in sufficient quantities, may produce all the effects of drunkenness.

OSCAR WILDE

These are my principles,
and if you don't like them...
well, I have others.

GROUCHO MARX

I hate being bi-polar.

It's really awesome.

The other day a man was going on about making vinegar out of leftover wine. But I got confused. What is leftover wine?

Alcohol will not solve your problems, but neither will water or milk.

I work so that I can afford
the amount of alcohol I need
to continue going to work.

Nothing makes sense before wine.

W.I.N.O.S.
Women In Need Of Sanity

To do is to be – Nietzsche

To be is to do – Kant

Do Be Do Be Do – Sinatra

Drink because you are happy, but never because you are miserable.

G.K. CHESTERTON

When all else fails,
drink wine.

Everything in moderation.
Especially moderation.

OSCAR WILDE

I hate it when I meow at cats and they don't meow back. Unbelievably rude.

The people who want to
stay in your life will
always find a way.

Sometimes when I am bored
I drink water,
just to shock my liver.

Reality is a hallucination
brought on by a lack
of alcohol.

Warning:
The consumption of alcohol
can lead to the impression
that people are laughing
with you.

It's not considered drinking alone if the cat is at home.

Hangover. God's way
of saying that you
kicked ass last night.

I've had a perfectly lovely evening. But this wasn't one of them.

GROUCHO MARX

Alcohol may be man's worst enemy, but the Bible says 'love your enemy.'

FRANK SINATRA

Clap along if you feel that happiness is the truth.

PHARRELL WILLIAMS

So you hate it when I am drunk. That's OK, because I hate you when I am sober.

When you are in jail,
a good friend will be trying to
bail you out. Your best friend
will be in there in the cell with
you saying: 'that was fun.'

GROUCHO MARX

Save water, drink wine.

Alcohol (n).
A bitter fluid used to help
white people dance.

Drink triple, see double,
and act single.

Roses are red,
violets are blue.
Wine is cheaper
than dinner for two.

I drink to make other people interesting.

GROUCHO MARX

Do not spoil what you have by desiring what you have not. Remember what you have now is once what you dreamed of.

EPICURUS

Colleague 1: 'You shouldn't drink while you are at work.'

Colleague 2: 'Oh don't worry, I'm not working right now.'

Warning:

The consumption of alcohol

may leave you wondering

what happened to

your clothes.

In wine there is wisdom.

In beer there is freedom.

In water there is bacteria.

Coffee keeps me going
until it's acceptable
to drink wine.

Ever felt like you have
had too much wine?
Me neither.

Men are like wine.
The best improve with age.

Warning:
drinking alcohol
before pregnancy can
cause pregnancy.

Life's too short to drink bad wine.

Where words fail,
wine speaks.

Remember, as far as everyone knows, you are a nice normal family.

The key to our lasting friendship is different taste in men and same taste in alcohol.

It's true that alcohol kills people. But how many people are born because of it?

I'm not really a
social drinker.
Most of my drinking
is work-related.

Work is the curse of the drinking class.

OSCAR WILDE

You look like I could
use a drink!

I once went years
without drinking.
And then I got
to drinking age.

Too much of a good thing
can be wonderful.

MAE WEST

I drink so that I cannot lie.

Happiness is a glass of
wine next to a fire.

I may be drunk, Miss,
but in the morning I shall
be sober and you will
still be ugly.

WINSTON CHURCHILL

The doctor said that
I needed to start drinking
more wine. Also, I'm
calling myself
'the doctor' now.

Trust me, you can dance.
– Wine

Wine does not make you fat. It makes you lean... lean against tables, walls and silly people.

I don't sing because
I am happy. I am happy
because I sing.

WILLIAM JAMES

It's a smile, it's a kiss,
it's a sip of wine,
it's summertime.

KENNY CHESNEY

Good friends know exactly
how many drinks you can
handle before you make
poor choices.

Children are great imitators. Give them something great to imitate.

I have finally
drunk enough wine
to tolerate you.
You may speak now.

Warning:
Excessive drinking can
lead to memory loss.
Or worse, memory loss.

Enjoy the little things in life, for one day you may look back and realise they were the big things.

I drink coffee because
I need it and wine because
I deserve it.

I'm not saying I did something terrible last night. But the devil woke up on my couch and he won't make eye contact with me.

I do yoga to relax.
Just kidding, I drink wine.

Wine is the best cure for birthdays.

I drink on Sundays to cope with the realisation that I am almost out of time to drink.

There's no wine in heaven,
we might as well drink
it here.

Those who were seen
dancing were thought
to be mad by those who
could not hear the music.

FRIEDRICH NIETZSCHE

Notes

Thoughts

Ideas

Dreams

Plans

Notes

Thoughts

Ideas

Dreams

Plans

Notes

Dreams

Plans

Notes

Thoughts

Ideas

Dreams

Schemes

Plans

MORE FROM ALLEGRA PUBLICATIONS

The Meaning of Coffee

The Meaning of Meow

The London Coffee Guide

The New York Coffee Guide

The Vienna Coffee Guide

The Belgium & Netherlands Coffee Guide

The London Cheese & Wine Guide

Great Cake Places

Allegra
PUBLICATIONS